Victorian and Edw

In 1812, Luddites (well-organised, armed ｐ .... and attacked factories that threatened their wa〉 ......, indeed, their livelihoods. Many were arrested and tried and seventeen of them were executed. The Luddites could not halt the relentless march of mechanisation and by the end of the 19th century Bradford had some two hundred mills and was the centre of Yorkshire's wool trade. With coal, iron and water in abundance, the town prospered and attracted businessmen and tourists.

Detailed guide books, such as Black's Guide to Yorkshire, were available to help visitors make the most of their stay. Black's was updated each year and included historical facts about towns and villages, where to stay, what to see and excursions to places of interest.

This booklet combines text relating to Bradford, Saltaire and Bingley (and their environs) from Black's Guide published in 1888, with photographs owned by the Keasbury-Gordon Photograph Archive.

It is in three parts. The first is fifty photographs, mostly taken between 1890 and 1930; the second, a detailed visitor's guide to Bradford and the third, a general history and description of Yorkshire. The text for parts two and three is reproduced from the 1888 guide-book. The map shows the road and railway network in the 1840s.

The Black's Guide text and the photographs complement each other and enable us to travel back in time to visit this important British town (now a city) at the height of its manufacturing power. I hope you enjoy the journey.

Andrew Gill

Bradford Alhambra Theatre

Bridge Street, Bradford

Forster Square, Bradford

Forster Square, Bradford

Forster Square, Bradford

Legrams Mill Disaster, 25th September, 1908

Manchester Road, Bradford

Manningham Lane, Bradford

Manningham Lane, Bradford

Bradford Market Hall

Market Street, Bradford

A tram accident, Bradford

Tyrrel Street, Bradford

Undercliffe, Bradford

Eastbrook Hall Wesleyan Mission, Bradford

Kirkgate Market, Bradford

A mobile advertisement for the 'Public Benefit Boot and
Shoe Company' outside Bradford Cemetery

A travelling cutler (knife sharpener) in Bradford

A Bradford street entertainer with a barrel organ

Sandwich board advertising in Bradford

Bingley Five Rise Locks on the Leeds and Liverpool Canal

Main Street towards Crossflatts, Bingley

Main Street, Bingley

Park Road, Bingley

Royal Hotel, Bingley

White Horse Inn, Bingley

Town Gate, Calverley

The tram terminus, Eccleshill

Eccleshill Co-op

Farsley Fire Brigade

Town Street, Farsley

Greengates

The Green, Idle

An Ox Roast, Town Gate, Idle

The Park, Pudsey

Church Lane, Pudsey

Lidget Hill, Pudsey

Lowtown, Pudsey

Pudsey Railway Station

Richardshaw Lane, Pudsey

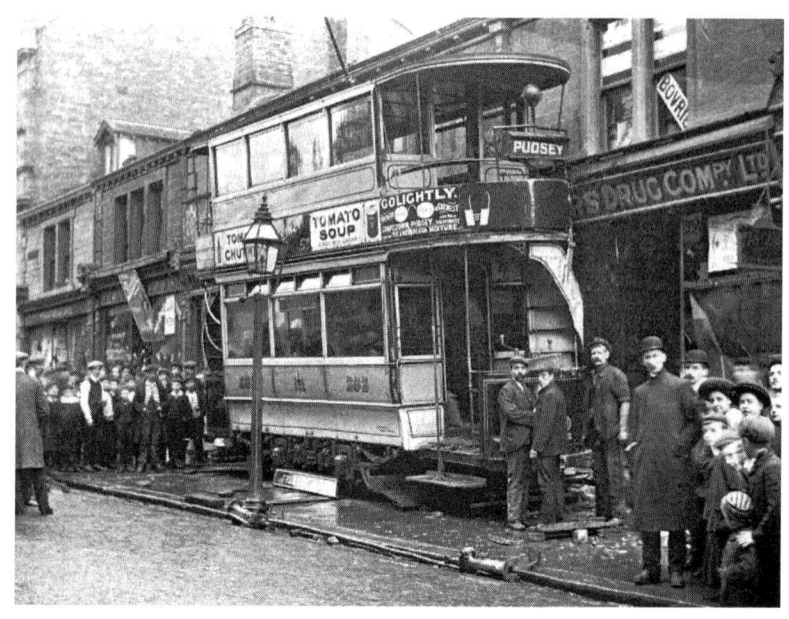

A tram accident in Pudsey

Gordon Terrace, Saltaire

Saltaire Railway Station

Briggate, Shipley

Otley Road, Shipley

Otley Road, Shipley

Carr Lane, Windhill, Shipley

Gaythorne Road, West Bowling

Wibsey High Street

Yeadon Aerodrome (now Leeds Bradford International Airport)

BRADFORD.

HOTELS.—*Midland* at the Midland Station (to be opened, 1889), *Alexandra,*
Victoria at Great Northern Station, *Talbot, George, Trevelyan.*

From Leeds 9 miles; from London, 195.

Bradford, one of the most important manufacturing towns
in Yorkshire, is finely situated at the union of three extensive
valleys. The name, according to antiquarians, is derived from a
broad ford over the small stream, a tributary of the Aire, on
which it is situated. The town does not seem to have been of
any note in ancient times, though the name occurs in some old
records. In the civil wars in the time of Charles I., Bradford
sided with the Parliament, and twice repulsed a large body of
the king's troops from the garrison of Leeds. It was afterwards
taken by the Earl of Newcastle. In 1812 occurred the disturb-
ances of the "Luddites," which resulted in the destruction of the
newly-introduced machinery in several mills, and in the convic-
tion and execution of seventeen of the rioters. A strike of
ten months' duration occurred in 1825, and was productive of
the usual unhappy effects. Since that date the history of Bradford
has been one of industry and prosperity, with occasional but not
frequent periods of commercial depression. In 1832 Bradford
obtained the privilege of returning two members to Parliament,
and in 1885 the number was increased to three.

The increase of this town in numbers and wealth since the
beginning of the century has been immense. Within the last
50 years the population has increased fourfold. In 1831 it
was 43,527; 1851, 103,778; 1871, 145,827; and in 1881,
194,495. In the beginning of the century there were only three

mills ; now there are nearly 200. The first steam-engine erected here was in 1798. It was only fifteen horse power. Now they are counted by hundreds, of every power and magnitude. The vast resources of nature which the neighbourhood enjoys, likewise contribute towards the trade and prosperity of the town. Coals and iron are found in abundance, and afford employment to thousands.

Bradford is the metropolis of the wool trade, to which merchants from Huddersfield, Halifax, and all parts of the clothing district resort for the purchase of the raw material. The chief manufactures are of worsted, alpaca, mohair, silk, and velvet.

THE PARISH CHURCH, which is dedicated to St. Peter, first claims the attention of the tourist. It is built in the Perpendicular style. The body of the fabric belongs to the time of Henry VI., but the tower is of a later date. The interior of the church has recently been entirely restored, the improvements including a fine oaken roof in the style of the building. The church contains many monuments, among which may be mentioned one to Abraham Sharpe, a celebrated mathematician, who died in 1742. A monument bearing a personification of Old Age, by Flaxman, erected to a gentleman of the name of Balme, will attract the attention of the visitor. There is also a fine sculptured font, with oak canopy.

The most important public building in the town is the TOWN HALL, completed in 1873, at a cost of £140,000, a very extensive and attractive edifice, which occupies an area of about 2000 square yards, in the centre of the borough. Its principal front is to Market Street, extending 275 feet in length. The tower, 220 feet high, which rises from behind a lofty gable, is designed after the campanile of the Palazzo Vecchio at Florence, while statues of the English sovereigns adorn the upper front of the building. The grand entrance is the most elaborately decorated portion of the hall, and on the staircase will be seen a fine picture illustrating the legend of the " Wild Boar of the Cliffe Wood." The interior of the edifice is devoted to the offices of the police department, town-council, and borough officials. The council-room, mayor's reception-room, and borough court-room, are planned with great consideration, and fitted up most handsomely. A very large clock, manufactured by Gillett and Bland, Croydon, is placed in the tower, and is supplied with some ingenious appliances. The carillon or musical machine plays every day one of twenty-one popular airs. The chimes, said to be the largest cast in Europe, consist of 13 bells, weighing 17 tons 9 cwts. In front of the Town Hall is a statue of Sir Titus Salt of Saltaire, opposite the Midland Station a statue to Richard Oastler, the Factory Act reformer, and in Peel Square a bronze statue of Sir Robert Peel, by Behnes.

St. George's Hall, in the Grecian style, was opened in 1853 for concerts and public meetings. The interior presents a very fine appearance, the hall being 152 feet long by 76 broad.

Among other public buildings may be mentioned the *Exchange* (containing a statue of Cobden), erected 1863 at a cost of nearly £30,000; the *Covered Markets* (1878); the new *Post Office*, in the Italian style, opposite the Midland Station, completed 1887; the *Art Gallery* and *Museum*, Darley Street (1879); the *Mechanics' Institute*, rebuilt 1871; the *Grammar School* (1653); the *Girls' Grammar School* (1875); and the *Technical College*, opened by the Prince and Princess of Wales in 1882. The Free Libraries Act was adopted in 1872, and district libraries established throughout the town. There are two theatres. Within recent years extensive street improvements have been carried out. Powers to borrow £300,000 for additional water-supply were obtained from Parliament in 1875, and works on a very extensive scale have been constructed.

Peel Park, 56 acres in extent, purchased by public subscription, was conveyed to the Corporation in 1863. *Lister Park*, 53 acres, was purchased from Mr. S. C. Lister for the comparatively small sum of £40,000; and in consideration of his generosity, the park was named Lister Park, and in 1875 his statue was erected in it. *Horton Park*, 39 acres, was opened in 1878; *Bowling Park*, 53 acres, in 1880; and *Bradford Moor Park* in 1884.

Tramways, begun in 1881, intersect the town in all directions.

Airedale Independent College is in the immediate vicinity of the town. There are also near Bradford academical institutions in connection with the Baptists and Wesleyan Methodists.

Saltaire, 4 miles from Bradford, by the side of the Aire (station on the Midland Railway), is one of the most remarkable achievements of the enterprise of this manufacturing age. The immense factory, which gives employment to upwards of 3000 persons, and the well-planned and complete little town in which many of the work-people reside, owe their existence to the energy and enterprise of the late Sir Titus Salt. *The Factory* is built of stone, in the Italian style, and covers an area of about 12 acres. Its main range runs from east to west. It is 550 feet long, 50 wide, 72 high, and consists of six stories. One great feature of this establishment is the manufacture of alpaca fabrics ; the late Sir Titus Salt, who was the first to introduce alpaca wool into the Bradford trade, having carried this branch to a high point of perfection. Besides alpaca, mohair, Russian, Botany, and other wools and silk are used in the manufacture of different fabrics, many of which are of great beauty.

The Town consists of handsome cottages, with wide and regular streets. A Jubilee Exhibition was held at Saltaire in 1887. As a memorial of the late Sir Titus Salt an Art School has been erected.

About three-quarters of a mile from Saltaire is SHIPLEY, another busy suburb of Bradford and a railway junction. The church is a prominently situated and respectable edifice.

BINGLEY, 2 miles beyond Saltaire by rail, is situated on a fine eminence near the Aire, and consists chiefly of one long street, built partly of brick and partly of stone. The parish had a population of 18,116 at the census of 1871. The principal manufacture is of woollens. The lordship of this place was bestowed by William the Conqueror on one of his followers, but nothing of any importance is recorded regarding the town in former times. A castle existed here two hundred and fifty years ago, on an elevation called the "Bailey Hill," but no traces of it now remain. The church is a plain structure of the time of Henry VIII., modernised in 1710. There are in this town several dissenting chapels and a free grammar school. The Prince of Wales' Park is situated on the eminence overlooking the town.

Near Baildon, 1½ miles from Shipley by rail, is *Baildon Hill*, a remarkable elevation overlooking the Aire. This hill is 922 feet high. Here there are ancient entrenchments and tumuli.

BOWLING, a mile and a half to the south of Bradford, was the headquarters of the Earl of Newcastle during the siege of Bradford. He resided in the Hall ; and there is a tradition that he was there dissuaded, by an apparition, from the bloody resolution to which he had come to give the inhabitants of Bradford to the sword. In the part of Bowling known as *Laister Dyke*, a very neat Gothic church, consisting of chancel, nave, and tower, was consecrated in 1861. Close at hand are the Bowling Iron Works, whence Government drew many supplies of war material during the Crimean campaign.

CALVERLEY, distant 3 miles (Midland Railway by Shipley), was the scene of "The Yorkshire Tragedy," a play which has been attributed (it is now agreed incorrectly) to Shakspere. The events on which the tragedy is founded took place at Calverley Hall in 1604. The hall was turned into separate tenements for a number of manufacturers in the early part of the present century.

At FULNECK, in the township of *Pudsey*, about five miles to the east, is a Moravian settlement, founded about 1748. The chief buildings are the hall, containing a chapel, a school for girls, and minister's dwelling ; a schoolhouse for boys ; a house for single men, another for single women, and another for widows. These buildings are situated on a terrace which commands a good prospect. Here James Montgomery the poet was educated. There are also houses for families. The chief employment of the inhabitants of this neat village is the woollen manufacture.

GENERAL DESCRIPTION
AND HISTORY OF THE COUNTY OF YORK.

YORKSHIRE is the largest county in England, exceeding by upwards of six hundred square miles the combined areas of Lincolnshire and Devonshire, which rank next to it in extent. In point of population it is inferior only to Lancashire and the metropolitan county of Middlesex. The outline is an irregular quadrangle, marked out by great natural boundaries. Its whole east side is washed by the German Ocean ; on the north, the Tees separates it from Durham ; on the south, the Humber divides it from Lincoln ; while a range of hills on the west almost exactly defines its limits towards Westmorland and Lancashire.

The lands of Yorkshire slope to the east and south, in accordance with their internal structure. With only one or two slight exceptions, such as the "Whinstone Dike" and "Whin Sill," the mineral masses are regularly stratified ; they are not, however, horizontal, but inclined to the eastward, receiving their axis of elevation from a great line of dislocation nearly coincident with the western boundary of the county. The surface of the county may be divided into distinctly-marked natural districts, each of which has superficial characteristics of scenery, as well as an internal formation, peculiarly its own. In the centre of the county, stretching from the Tees to the Humber, is the great Vale of York, a beautiful and fertile tract upon the New Red Sandstone series, bordered on the east by the Lias, and on the west by the

Gunnerside in Swaledale

Magnesian Limestone. The bold and picturesque scenery of the western hills and dales is due to the harder rocks of the Millstone Grit series and the Scar Limestone, which here come to the surface. In the south-western part of the county we have a considerable tract of the Coal formation, the site of the great manufacturing towns of the West Riding, and densely peopled throughout. The north-eastern district is of the Oolitic and Lias formations; and the south-eastern district, with its smooth green wolds, is of Chalk. Between these districts lies the Vale of Pickering, which in prehistoric times was either a river course or a lake opening to the sea. The formation of this tract is of Kimmeridge clay, covered by lacustrine and river deposits. In the portion of the south-eastern district, which is called Holderness, the chalk gives place to a perishable formation of sand, gravel, clay, and lake and river sediment, on which the sea makes constant and easy encroachments.

"The main external features of Yorkshire," says Professor Phillips, " are strictly explicable on the simplest possible theory : viz., that of the long continued action of the agitated sea on the strata which composed its bed, at the time when this bed was raised to constitute land. These strata, by their various degrees of consolidation and peculiarities of position, offered unequal resistance to the waves, and have been unequally wasted ; the softer strata, which suffered most waste, have left the greatest hollows—the red marls and blue lias having been excavated in the Vale of York, the Kimmeridge clays in the Vale of Pickering, the limestone shales in Craven, and the tertiary sands in Holderness ; while harder masses of chalk constitute the wolds, oolites and sandstones form the moorlands of Whitby, still firmer sandstones and limestones, with some slaty and some basaltic masses, constitute the higher regions of the west.

"To geological differences on a large scale we thus clearly trace the main distinctive features of the great natural divisions of Yorkshire. The mineral qualities and positions of rocks, with the accidents to which they have been subjected, give us the clue to the forms of mountains and valleys, the aspect of waterfalls and rocks, the prevalent herbage, and the agricultural appropriation. Even surface colour and pictorial effect are not fully understood without geological inquiry. While limestone 'scars' support a sweet green turf, and slopes of shale give a stunted growth of bluish sedge, gritstone ' edges' are often deeply covered by brown heath, and abandoned to grouse, the sportsman, or the peat-cutter. In a word, geological distinctions are nowhere more boldly marked than in Yorkshire, or more constantly in harmony with the other leading facts of physical geography."

Perhaps no county in England possesses such varied and interesting scenery, whether sea-coast or inland. From the lofty summits of Mickle Fell, Whernside, Ingleborough, and the other hills in the western range, down to the level and extensive Vale of York, and eastward to the chalk wolds over the Humber, the high moors above the Esk, and the indented sea-coast beyond, there is a succession of scenery presenting every order of beauty, from the wildest sublimity to the gentlest loveliness. The dales of Yorkshire are acknowledged to be unequalled by any others in the kingdom; and some of them, in the more remote parts of the county, present, both in their scenery and their inhabitants, attractions of no ordinary kind to the adventurous tourist.

The climate, like the soil, varies in different places. The western moors and dales have a bracing climate, the cold being more severe than on the eastern heights. The climate of the central part of the county is equable and healthy. The highest points are Mickle Fell, in the north-west angle of the county, 2600 feet above the sea; Whernside, 2384; Ingleborough, 2361; and other hills of rather less altitude in the west; and Burton Head, 1485, in the north-east. The waters of Yorkshire, with the exception of that very small part of the county on the west slope of the Pennine chain which is drained by the Ribble, all find their way to the eastern sea at points within the limits of the county. The principal rivers unite in the Humber. They are—the Don, Calder, Aire, Wharfe, Nid, Ure, Swale, Derwent, and Hull. The Esk has its own outfall to the sea, as has also the Tees, which forms the northern boundary of the county.

The earliest inhabitants of Yorkshire, of whom we have any record, were the Brigantes, one of the most powerful British tribes. Their territories appear to have included Yorkshire and Lancashire, with perhaps portions of the neighbouring counties. Cartismandua, who delivered up the heroic Caractacus to the Romans, A. D. 51, was queen of this tribe. This action probably conciliated the Romans for a time; for the Brigantes were not reduced under the power of that nation till the reign of

Vespasian, in the year 71. When Constantine divided Britain into three parts, Yorkshire was included in *Maxima Cæsariensis.* Under the Saxons it formed part of the kingdom of Northumberland, having the name of Deira, when that kingdom was divided into two parts. Along with the rest of the kingdom of Northumbria, Yorkshire yielded to Egbert, king of the West Saxons, about the year 827. On the invasion of the Danes, Yorkshire was reduced after some sanguinary conflicts, in one of which the rival Saxon kings, Osbert and Ella, too late in uniting against the common foe, were slain at York, in 867. Seventy years later, Athelstan " of earls the lord, of heroes the bracelet giver," defeated the Danes in a bloody battle, and brought Northumbria again under Saxon rule. Again and again the Danes renewed the contest, as their fleets landed fresh troops of hardy Northmen on the English coast. The last great struggle was fought in 1066. Hadrada, king of Norway, entered the Humber with 500 ships, and landed an army, which, with that of the Danish prince Tosti, who had invited him, amounted to 60,000 men. Marching upon York, the invaders speedily took it by storm. Harold, the Saxon king of England, at once marched towards York to oppose the invaders, who withdrew, and took up a strong position at Stamford Brig. The dauntless Harold at once attacked them. The battle raged from seven in the morning till three in the afternoon, and issued in the death of Hadrada and Tosti, and the almost total destruction of their army. Three weeks later, Harold had to resist another invader; and the "last of the Saxons" perished on the field of Hastings. William the Conqueror pursued the same policy towards Yorkshire as towards the rest of the kingdom. He garrisoned York, and bestowed the castles and manors throughout the county on his followers. Several risings against the Norman power, which took place in this county, were punished with great severity. The first parliament mentioned in history, was held in York, by Henry II., in 1160. Many of the principal facts in the history of the county after this period fall to be noticed in that of its chief city, which continued for a long period to be the scene of many of the most important events in our national history. During the wars of the Roses, Yorkshire was the scene of various important struggles, the chief of which were the battles of Wakefield in 1460, and of Towton in 1461. The suppression of monastic houses by Henry VIII. gave rise to a serious rebellion, commonly called the "Pilgrimage of Grace," in 1536. Several smaller risings occurred shortly after this period; but they were easily and summarily suppressed. Yorkshire was the theatre of many struggles between the royalists and parliamentarians. It was at Marston Moor that the important battle was fought which gave a blow to the fortunes of the haughty and unfortunate Charles, from which they never recovered. With the exception of some royal visits, and several risings in the manufacturing districts, occasioned by commercial distress and the introduction of machinery, the subsequent history of this county presents no events deserving special notice.

Yorkshire contains numerous remains of the peoples who have successively ruled it. The Brigantes or Highlanders—that being the meaning of their name—have left traces of themselves in the names of many of the rivers, and some of the mountains and ancient sites of population; in their tumuli, containing bones, weapons, and ornaments, to be seen on the Wolds and elsewhere; in their camps, such as antiquarians trace at Barwick in Elmet, Hutton Ambo, and Langton; in their stone monuments; and in their pottery.

The Romans have left very numerous and distinct memorials of themselves. Their military roads traverse the county in various directions. One great line enters Yorkshire near Bawtry, crosses the Don at Doncaster (*Danum*), the Aire at Castleford (*Legeolium*), and the Wharfe at Tadcaster (*Calcaria*), and reaches York (*Eboracum*), whence it passes in a north-westerly direction to Aldborough (*Isurium*), then to Catterick Bridge (*Cataractonium*), where it crosses the Swale, and passing still north, leaves the county by crossing the Tees at Pierse Bridge. A little to the north of Catterick, a branch of the road goes off to the left to Greta Bridge, whence it proceeds towards Carlisle. From Eboracum, a road in many places well marked goes eastward by *Derventio* (Malton) and *Delgovitia*, to *Praetorium* (Dunsley). From Isurium several lines of road branch off; one, very distinctly marked, proceeding in a south-westerly direction, crossing the Nid, Wharfe, and Aire, and following the course of the Ribble towards Preston. Roman camps are numerous. The earliest of their stations appears to have been at Aldborough. Traces, more or less distinct, may be seen of camps at York, Bainbridge, Catterick Bridge, Greta Bridge, Stainmoor, Malton, and Cawthorne; while the names and positions of numerous other places, taken in conjunction with the geography of Ptolemy and the itineraries of Antoninus, make it evident that they were Roman settlements. Relics of the Romans have been frequently found, in the shape of votive altars, stone coffins, pavements, sculptures, coins, ornaments of glass, coral, bronze, gold and silver, etc.*

The Anglo-Saxons and Danes are not without their monuments. These are chiefly mounds, raised either for defence or as memorials for the fallen brave. Warlike weapons and ornaments of various kinds have been found in these mounds. The remains of Saxon architecture which Yorkshire possesses consist chiefly of a few pillars, arches, and inscriptions, preserved by being incorporated with later structures. These, which are chiefly in churches, are very interesting. Norman remains are more numerous, and are to be found in much purity and perfection in various castles and ecclesiastical edifices. There are many old fortresses in this county, which are interesting alike for the antiquity of their erection and their historical associations. Its stately minsters, still preserved in their old magnificence, its ancient churches, and the grand ruins of its crumbling abbeys, present abundant and excellent materials for a study and comparison of the different orders of architecture.

This extensive county has given to the world many eminent names. The principal natives of Yorkshire who figure prominently in public affairs, in ancient times, are : Richard Plantagenet, third Duke of York, whose ambition and fate are

---

* EARLY INHABITANTS.—The researches in the tumuli of the wolds and moors, conducted through several years by the Rev. Canon Greenwell of Durham, and with him Sir John Lubbock, Bart. (author of *Pre-Historic Times*); John Evans, Esq., F.R.S., F.S.A., of Hemel Hempstead ; Mr. Monkman, Malton ; and the Rev. Fred. Porter, Yedingham, have shown that in prehistoric times two races of people inhabited Yorkshire. The earlier race (so thought) was peculiar for long heads (dolicho-cephalic), and buried in long barrows mostly, and had the plainest of pottery, and nothing but stone or flint weapons and implements. Another race, of round heads (brachy-cephalic), buried in round barrows, had a knowledge of metal, implements of bronze being found with their interments, along with ornate pottery and flint implements. The Rev. Canon Greenwell has published a work on the prehistoric people, under the title *A Decade of Skulls from Ancient Northumbria*. Recent excavations at Ulrome, near Driffield, have brought to light an extensive prehistoric lake-dwelling, with some implements of a previously unknown type.

celebrated by Shakspere in "King Henry VI. ;" Richard Scroop, also immortalized by Shakspere, beheaded for high treason in 1405 ; John Fisher, Bishop of Rochester, and afterwards Cardinal, born in 1458, and beheaded, for his opposition to Henry VIII., in 1535 ; Sir William Gascoigne, the chief justice who committed Prince Henry to prison for contempt of court, born 1350, died 1413 ; Sir William de la Pole, founder of the powerful family of Suffolk—the character of the fourth Earl and first Duke of which family is delineated in "King Henry VI., Part II."—died 1356 ; Andrew Marvell, the friend of Milton, and the consistent and unswerving advocate of constitutional principles, born 1620, died 1678. In later times, Hull, the place which Andrew Marvell represented in Parliament, has given birth to William Wilberforce, the friend of the slave, and returned him as its representative. He was born in 1759, and died in 1833. Of noted commanders Yorkshire claims—Thomas, Lord Fairfax, the famous parliamentary general, born 1611, died 1671 ; Sir John Lawson, the celebrated admiral, died in action, after a brilliant career, 1665 ; Sir Martin Frobisher, knighted for his gallantry in an action with the Spaniards, and killed in an attack on Brest, 1594. Several noted travellers were born in this county : Armigel Waad, styled by Fuller, "the English Columbus," the first Englishman who set foot on the shores of America, died in 1568 ; Sir Thomas Herbert, who explored many parts of Asia and Africa, and published an account of his travels, was born in 1606, and died in 1682 ; and Captain James Cook, the circumnavigator of the globe, born 1728, killed by the savages at the Sandwich Islands, 1779.

In literature, Yorkshire presents a vast array of names. Alcuin, the most distinguished scholar of his age, and the friend of Charlemagne, was born about 735, and died 804. Other natives celebrated for their learning are—Roger Ascham, the tutor of Queen Elizabeth, died 1568 ; Sir Henry Saville, an accomplished Greek scholar, and the founder of two professorships at Oxford, born 1549, died 1622 ; Dr. Joseph Hill, editor of Schrevelius' Lexicon, born 1625, died 1707 ; Richard Bentley, the celebrated classical critic, born 1661, died 1742 ; John Potter, Archbishop of Canterbury, author of the "Antiquities of Greece," born 1674, died 1747 ; Dr. Conyers Middleton, author of the "Life of Cicero," "Letter from Rome," etc., born 1683, died 1750. Several natives of this county have taken a high place as topographical historians and antiquarians by their works upon different districts of it. The chief names are those of Roger Dodsworth (1585-1654), Ralph Thoresby (1658-1725), Thomas Gent (1691-1778), Dr. Burton (1697-1771), Francis Drake (died 1770), Dr. Young, Rev. J. Hunter, Rev. J. Graves, Rev. J. Tickell, T. Hinderwell, Rev. W. Eastmead, Rev. C. Wellbeloved, G. Poulson, Professor Phillips, John Browne, J. Walbran, etc.* In an enumeration of writers on divinity belonging to this county, an honoured place must be given to John de Wycliffe, "the Morning Star of the Reformation," and the translator of the Bible, born about 1324, died 1384 ; and to Miles Coverdale, the English reformer, born 1499, died 1580. More recent are— Matthew Pool, author of the "Synopsis Criticorum," a classic in biblical interpretation, born 1624, died 1679 ; John Tillotson, Archbishop of Canterbury, whose "Sermons" hold a high place among the literature of the pulpit, born 1630, died 1694 ; Joseph Bingham, author of the "Origines Ecclesiasticae," born 1668, died 1723 ; Beilby Porteous, Bishop of London, author of a "Life of Archbishop Slaker," and various works in theology, and of some elegant poems, born 1731, died 1808 ; Joseph Milner, author of a valuable "History of the Church of Christ," born 1744, died 1820 ; John Pye Smith, D.D., author of "The Scripture Testimony to the Messiah," and other works, born 1775, died 1850. Next let us notice the men of science :—John Smeaton, civil engineer, the architect of Eddystone Lighthouse, was born in 1724, and died in 1792 ; Joseph Priestley, author of numerous works on experimental philosophy and other subjects, born 1733, died 1804 ; John Ellerton Stocks, M.D., a noted botanist, born 1820, died 1854 ; Professor Sedgwick, of Cambridge University, author of "A Synopsis of the Classification of the Palæozoic Rocks," was born about the year 1786. Yorkshire has produced a fair number of poets, though none of them stand in the highest rank. We take the principal names, in the order of time : John Gower, called by Bale "poet laureate," and said to have been the instructor of Chaucer, was the author of various works, written, some in English, others in French and Latin, died in 1402 ; George Sandys, translator of Ovid's Metamorphoses— a work to which Pope declares that English poetry owes much,

* Dr. Thomas Whitaker, the Dugdale of Yorkshire, was not a native of the county, being born in Norfolk in 1759. One or two of the latest of the names enumerated above may also belong to other counties.

was born in 1577, and died in 1643 ; Edward Fairfax, the translator of Tasso, died in 1632 ; Sir Robert Stapleton, the translator of Juvenal and other classic poets, and author of some dramatic pieces, died in 1669 ; William Congreve, the dramatist, was born in 1669, and died in 1729 ; Sir Samuel Garth, author of "The Dispensary," and other poems, was born in 1671, and died in 1718 ; William Mason, best known by his dramatic poem of "Caractacus," and his biography of the poet Gray, was born in 1725, and died in 1797 ; Ebenezer Elliott, the "Corn-Law Rhymer," born 1781, died 1849 ; Herbert Knowles, best known by his exquisite "Lines written in the Churchyard of Richmond," died at the early age of nineteen, born 1797, died 1816 ; Monckton Milnes, M.P., author of "Memorials of a Tour in Greece," and three volumes of poems, born 1809. In other departments of literature are—David Hartley, author of "Observations on Man," born 1705, died 1757 ; John Foster, author of "Essays in a series of Letters," an "Essay on the Evils of Popular Ignorance," etc., born 1770, died 1839 ; the late Earl of Carlisle, author of a "Diary in Turkish and Greek Waters," born 1802 ; Edward Baines, M.P., author of a "History of the Cotton Manufacture," born 1806. Several names of novelists occur, all of them females : Mrs. Hofland, author of "The Son of a Genius," and numerous works for the young, born 1770, died 1844 ; the Brontës —Charlotte, author of "Jane Eyre," "Shirley," and "Vilette," born 1816, died 1855—Emily, author of "Wuthering Heights," born 1819, died 1848—and Agnes, author of "Agnes Grey," and "The Tenant of Wildfell Hall," born 1822, died 1849 ; Mrs. Gaskell, the biographer of Miss Brontë, and author of "Ruth," "North and South," and other works ; Miss Pardoe, author of "The City of the Sultan," "The Romance of the Harem," and numerous other works. To Yorkshire belong the painters— Benjamin Wilson, who flourished about 1760 ; William Kent, born 1685, died 1748 ; John Jackson, born 1778, died 1831 ; William Etty, R.A., born 1787, died 1849 ; and W. P. Frith, born 1819 ; the sculptor, John Flaxman, born 1755, died 1826 ; the engraver, William Lodge, born 1649, died 1689 ; and the actor, Richard John Smith, of the Adelphi, born 1786, died 1855.

The area of Yorkshire is 6067 square miles, or 3,882,851 statute acres. The population, according to the census of 1861, amounted to 2,033,610, and at the subsequent censuses as follows :—

DIVISION.	Area in acres.	Pop. in 1871.	Pop. in 1881.	Persons to acre.	
				1871.	1881.
North Riding .	1,361,664	293,278	346,260	0·22	0·25
East Riding .	750,828	268,466	315,460	0·36	0·42
West Riding .	1,768,380	1,830,815	2,175,314	1·03	1·23
City of York .	1,979	43,796	49,530	22·13	25·03
Total of County	3,882,851	2,436,355	2,886,564	0·63	0·74

In 1881 the total number of males was 1,420,001, and of females 1,466,563—the males exceeding the females in the North Riding by 3534.

The county is divided into four parts—viz. the three *Ridings* and the *Ainsty* of York. For parliamentary purposes the West Riding is subdivided into three districts—East returning 6 members, North 5, and South 8. The North Riding returns 4 members, and the East Riding 3. Bradford returns 3 members, Dewsbury 1, Halifax 2, Huddersfield 1, Hull 3, Leeds 5, Middlesbrough 1, Pontefract 1, Scarborough 1, Sheffield 5, Wakefield 1, and York 2. The North Riding contains an area of 2128 square miles, or 1,361,664 acres, and 346,260 persons. The occupations are chiefly agricultural, but mines employ upwards of 8000 persons. The total number of members returned from this Riding is 8. The East Riding, taking along with it the city of York, has an area of 1176 square miles, or 752,807 acres, and a population of 364,990. In this part of the county the number of persons employed in agriculture is almost equal to that of those engaged in every kind of manufacture. Cotton and flax, engines and ships, are the chief manufactures. The total number of members returned by this division of the county is 5. The West Riding is the most important part of the county in point of manufactures and commerce. Its extent is 2763 square miles, or 1,768,380 acres ; and its population, 2,175,314. This is the great seat of the woollen and iron manufactures, of which details are given under the principal towns where the manufactures are carried on.

Agriculture is in a medium state of improvement, but is regarded as not so advanced as in Northumberland and Lincolnshire. Yorkshire, however, is more a grazing than an agricultural county. Craven, and the upper parts of the West Riding generally, are purely pastoral, there being scarcely any arable land in cultivation in this Riding, except in the lower districts. In the East Riding and the lower parts of the North Riding there are considerable tracts of good arable ground. Farms are generally small, and let at high rents from year to year. The total number of farmers in Yorkshire, according to the census of 1881, was 27,647; of whom 25,232 were males, and 2215 females. Farm labourers were reckoned at 61,861; 58,738 being males, and 3123 females. All these figures show a marked decline in the last twenty years. Cattle are mostly of the short-horned breed; but there are large numbers of long-horns, and many varieties produced by crosses of these two breeds. Sheep are numerous, and also of different breeds. Yorkshire has long been celebrated for its horses. Many of the most noted racers which have appeared on the turf were bred and trained in this county. The Cleveland bays are highly esteemed as carriage horses. Horses for agricultural and general purposes are bred in great numbers in this county; and the horse fairs which are held here at stated times are frequented by dealers from all parts of the kingdom, as well as by foreigners.

The mineral productions of Yorkshire are—coal in abundance, iron, lead, copper, alum, slate, limestone (some of it equal, if not superior, to the Derbyshire marble), building stone, etc. There are very valuable mineral waters in various parts of the county. Those of Harrogate and Scarborough have been long celebrated, and are much resorted to.

The East Riding, though containing the important port of Hull, is chiefly dependent on agriculture, and on the attractions of the beautiful watering-places extending along the coast. Until 1850 the North Riding was even less famed for its manufacturing industry, but the discovery of the rich iron ores in the Cleveland and Hambleton districts wrought a complete transformation in its prospects. While mining villages have sprung up in all directions, the town and port of Middlesbrough has been created; other towns have increased with almost unexampled rapidity; and Redcar and Saltburn have developed into fashionable seaside resorts. The great centre of Yorkshire industry is, however, in the West Riding, the foundation of its prosperity being the coal and iron field stretching from Leeds on the north to Sheffield in the south. But while iron and steel are the staple industries of Sheffield, and are extensively manufactured in other towns, it is for its woollen and worsted manufactures that the West Riding is chiefly celebrated. The West Riding has almost a monopoly of the worsted manufactures of the United Kingdom. The manufacturing district may be said, roughly, to include the whole of Yorkshire south of the Aire from Leeds to Skipton. It is deeply indented by valleys which originally supplied abundance of water for the mills, but now this is largely supplemented by steam-worked machinery, for which the proximity of immense coal supplies is a great advantage.

About the Author, Andrew Gill: I live in Lancashire, England and have collected early photographs and optical antiques for over forty years. I am a professional 'magic lantern' showman presenting lantern shows and giving talks on Victorian optical entertainments for museums, festivals, special interest groups and universities. I am the owner of the Keasbury-Gordon Photograph Archive.

The photograph captions in this album are those printed or hand-written on the original slides or photographs. If you think they are inaccurate or if you have relevant information that I can include in future editions, please contact me.

To purchase prints of selected historical photographs from my archive, visit www.the-keasburygordon-photograph-archive.artistwebsites.com

For a licence to use my historical photographs for commercial purposes, please contact me.

For information about magic lanterns and slides, visit the website of the Magic Lantern Society: www.magiclantern.org.uk

To contact me, email lanternist@ntlworld.com

I have published historical booklets and photo albums on the subjects below. They are available as printed books and ebooks from Amazon. To view all titles, search amazon for 'andrew gill booklets', then click the 'Andrew Gill' link under any title.

Ancient Baalbec   *Ancient Palmyra*   Birkenhead, Port Sunlight and the Wirral   *Birmingham*   Ballyclare May Fair   *Blackpool*   Bournemouth   *Brighton*   Brixham and Dartmouth   *Burnley's Trams*   Cornwall: Morwenstow to Tintagel   *Cumberland*   CWS Crumpsall Biscuit Factory   *Dawlish, Teignmouth and Newton Abbot*   Doncaster   *Eastbourne*   Edinburgh   *Egypt's Ancient Monuments*   Fife   *First World War*   Forth Railway Bridge   *Franco-British 'White City' London Exhibition of 1908*

16640886R00027

Printed in Great Britain
by Amazon